GERTIE

THE FEARLESS

Gertie the Fearless

Ann Coleridge

Modern Curriculum Press

Cleveland and Toronto

illustrated by Mark Payne

Gertie Fogle is a very important lady.

6   Each morning and each afternoon,
     she controls the traffic
     with a wave of her hand.

One day, she noticed two suspicious-looking men watching her.

Perhaps they meant to pounce on her
and steal her bus money.

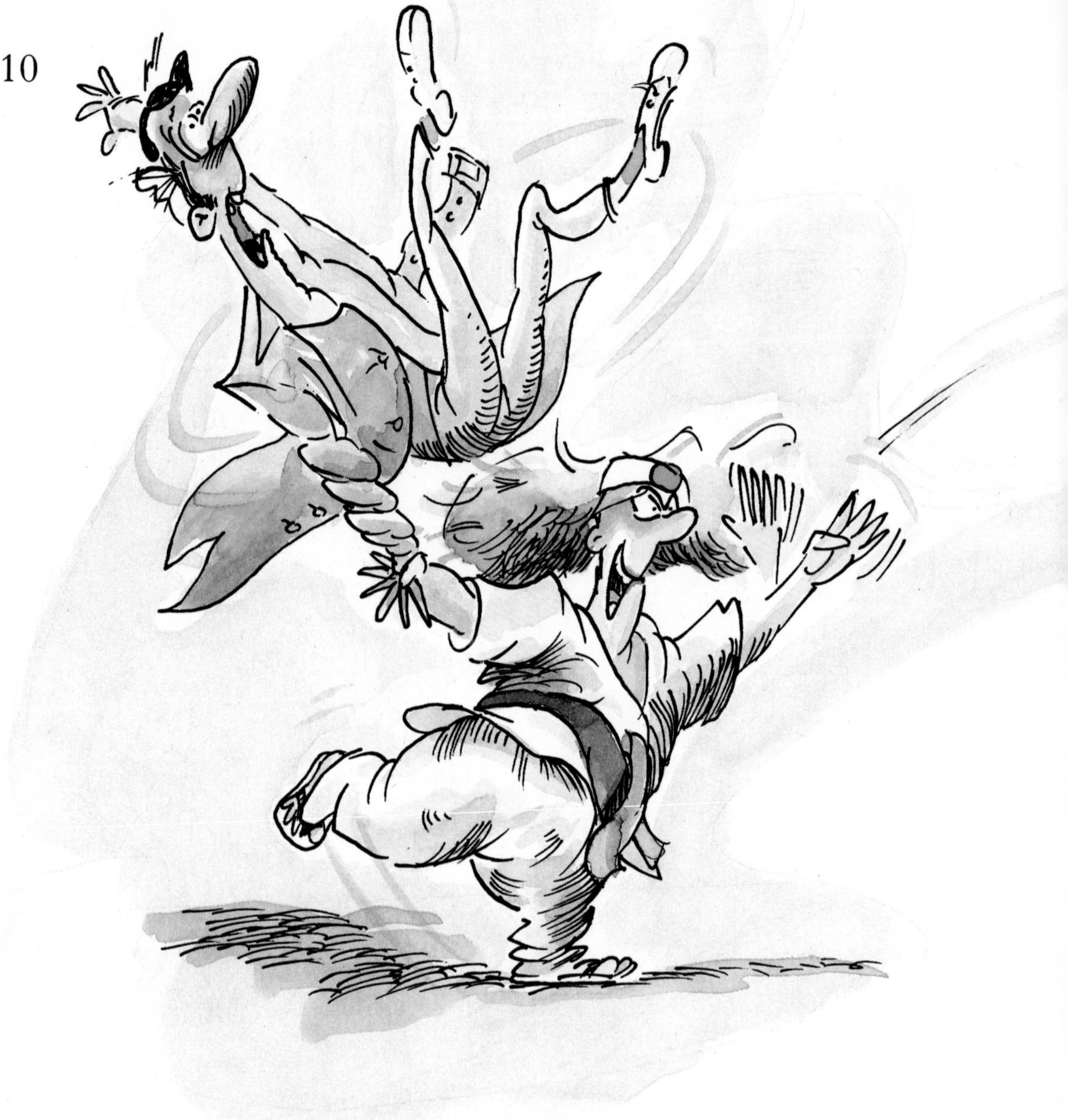

If they did,
Gertie would soon deal with them.

But the men didn't pounce on her.

The next day,
the men were there again.
Perhaps they were planning
to kidnap one of the children.

If they did,
Gertie would soon deal with them.

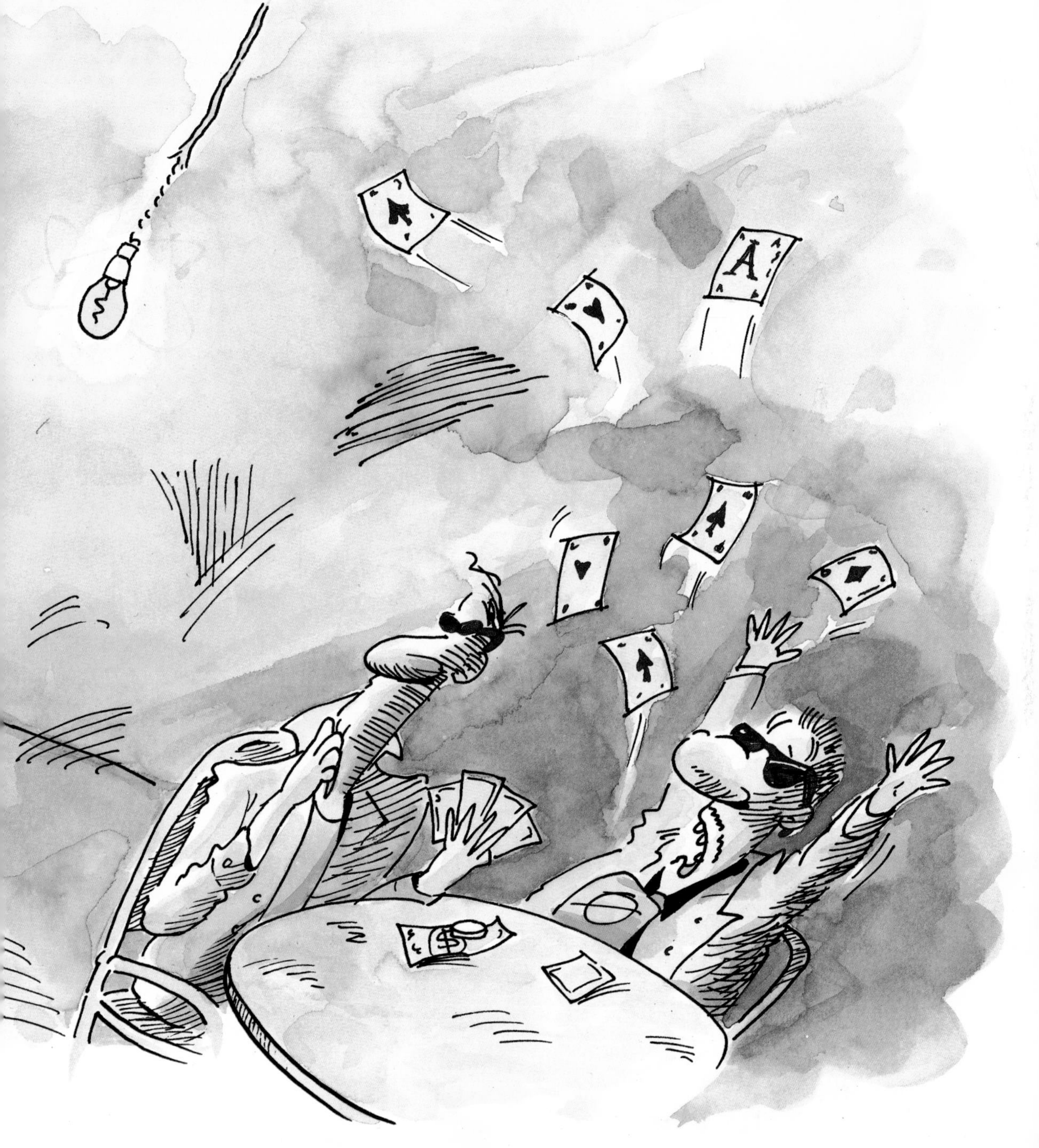

But the men didn't kidnap anybody.

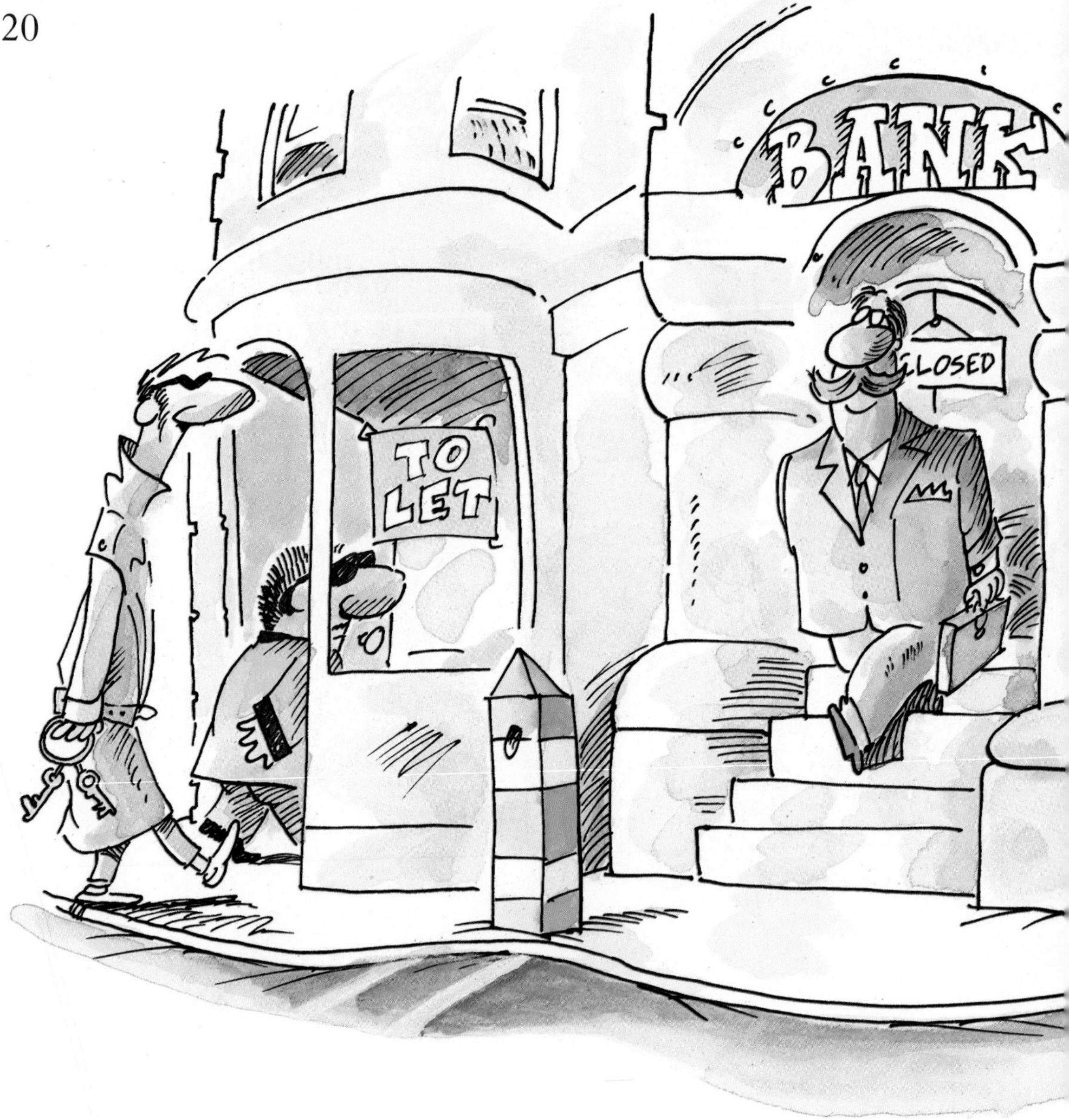
BANK
CLOSED
TO LET

The next day,
the men were there again.
Perhaps they were going to dig a tunnel
from the empty shop to the bank next door
and steal all the money.

If they did,
Gertie would soon deal with them.

But the men didn't rob the bank.

The next day,
the men were there again.
Gertie decided
that they were quite nice after all.

Early the next day,
the bank was robbed.

"Well, who would have believed it?" said Gertie.